Practical Guide to the Operational Use of the TT-33 Tokarev Pistol

By Erik Lawrence

Copyright ©2014 Erik Lawrence

ATTENTION US MILITARY UNITS, US GOVERNMENT AGENCIES AND PROFESSIONAL ORGANIZATIONS: Quantity discounts are available on bulk purchases of this book. Special books or book excerpts can also be created to fit specific needs. For information, please contact:

Erik Lawrence
www.vig-sec.com   erik@vig-sec.com

Although the author and publisher have made every effort to ensure the accuracy and completeness of information contained in this book, we assume no responsibility for the use or misuse of information contained in this book .errors, inaccuracies, omissions, or any inconsistency herein. Portions of this manual are excerpts from outside sources but have been validated and modified as necessary.

Printed and bound in the United States of America

First printing 2011
Second printing 2014

ISBN-10: 1-941998-07-0
ISBN-13: 978-1-941998-07-6
EBOOK – ISBN-13: 978-1-941998-26-7
LCCN: Not yet assigned

Firearms are potentially dangerous and must be handled responsibly by individuals. The technical information presented in this publication on the use of the TT-33 Tokarev pistol reflects the author's research, beliefs, and experiences. The information in this book is presented for academic study only. Neither the author nor the publisher assumes any responsibility for the use or misuse of information contained in this book.

SAFETY NOTICE - Before starting an inspection, ensure the weapon is cleared. Do not manipulate the trigger until the weapon has been cleared of all ammunition. Inspect the chamber to ensure that it is empty and no ammunition is present. Keep the weapon oriented in a safe direction when loading and handling.

AMMUNITION NOTICE - This weapon fires the 7.62x25mm, not the 9x19mm NATO (9mm Luger) or 9x18mm (Makarov). Firing the incorrect ammunition will damage the weapon and possibly injure the operator.

PROPER TRAINING - Training should be received from knowledgeable and experienced operators on this particular weapons system. Vigilant Security Services, LLC provides this training and continually perfects its instruction with up-to-date information from actual use.

www.vig-sec.com

PREFACE

This manual is intended to be a reference for those involved in the use, maintenance and instruction of the featured firearm. My aim in writing these manuals is to set the record straight and dispel many of the false assumptions related to the different firearms. The early sections of the manual contain background material on the featured firearm which allows the user to gain the basic building blocks for further education. The firearms featured in these manuals have been used for decades by our allies and enemies, and will be for the foreseeable future, so why are we not experts with them? If I am fighting with the firearm or providing instruction on a firearm, I want to use and know their system better than they do.

The rationale for writing these manuals comes from the fact that there are not libraries of easily accessible references to use in developing your own training system for these firearms. Many of the old military field manuals are decades old and were incorrectly translated by someone who had no idea what the firearm could do, let alone basic firearm knowledge. We started from the ground up and developed the manuals to provide instruction in progressive steps that could be easily grasped and continually referred back to. A good grounding in the basics of firearms, safety, and instruction allows the user to use these manuals to their maximum value. A competent user will find little difficulty in interpreting and applying the information in the manual to their own training program.

The guide goes through the most fundamental parts of the firearm in detail and more advanced techniques are not covered as extensively. With this in mind the user can use these principles and adapt it as needed to their required level of instruction. The emphasis of this guide is in acquiring familiarity with the fundamentals of all firearms and learned competence rather than becoming a firearms guru.

Many of the points in these guides were developed from scratch in theatres of conflict and are continually improved and updated for each edition. I have continually used vetted points from users and professionals in the guides to continually update them to the best known practices for each particular firearm. If it is valid and relevant we will include it in the next edition.

Please note that this guide assumes some familiarity with the basic concepts in firearm safety, gun handling skills, common sense and an ability to process new information. Readers should have knowledge of the difference in calibers, countries of origin, and the knowledge of the priority of the skills needed for development.

I hope you find this work useful and remember that a manual does not replace proper training and hands on experience. Please email comments to erik@vig-sec.com, particularly if you find any errors or glaring omissions.

Erik Lawrence

Table of Contents

TT-33

Tokarev

Section 1

Introduction

The objective of this manual is to allow the reader to be able to use the TT-33 pistol competently. The manual will give the reader background/specifications of the weapon; instructions on its operation, disassembly, and assembly; proper firing procedure; and malfunction/misfire procedures. Operator-level maintenance will also be detailed to allow the reader to understand and become competent in the use and maintenance of the TT-33 pistol.

Description

The Tokarev TT-33 (*Tokarev-Tula 1933*) is a blowback-operated, single-action pistol with a steel frame and steel slide construction. Externally, the TT-33 is very similar to John Browning's blowback-operated FN Model 1903 automatic pistol, but it also used Browning's short recoil dropping-barrel system from the M1911. However, the TT-33 is not a 1911 clone as it employs a much simpler hammer/sear assembly with an external hammer.

The TT-33 is chambered for the 7.62x25mm Tokarev cartridge, which was itself based on the similar 7.63x25mm Mauser cartridge used in the Mauser C96 pistol. Able to withstand tremendous abuse, large numbers of the TT-33 were produced during WWII and well into the 1950s. The TT-33 replaced the Nagant revolver and was widely used by Soviet troops during World War II..

The TT-33 was an improved design of the TT-30, which was the first major-employed automatic pistol in the Soviet forces, but few TT-30s were built before the update in 1933. The TT-30 was developed in the early 1930s by Fedor Tokarev as a service pistol for the Soviet military to replace the Nagant M1895 revolver that had been in use since czarist times.

The single-action trigger has no manual safety except for the pistols imported to the US on which ATF mandated one, other than the half-cock notch on the hammer. The safety visible on the left of the frame was fitted to comply with the BATF rules requiring an external safety on imports. In fact, the normal safety of the TT-33 is the half-cock notch. The retrofitted safety should not be relied on for cocked and locked carry. You should choose to only carry the TT with an empty chamber; if not you will need to rely on the half-cock notch. The hammer unit was made as a single unit, easily detachable for cleaning and maintenance. Fixed sights were factory zeroed for 25 meters. Grip panels were usually made of plastic or wood (wartime production).

Figure 1-1 Tokarev TT-33, post-WWII manufacture (with smaller slide serrations)

The characteristics of the Tokarev TT-33 pistol

    A.   Country of Origin: USSR/Russia

    B.   Military Designation: TT-33

    C.   Cartridge Type: 7.62mm X 25mm Tokarev cartridge

    D.   Type of Feed: 8-round box magazine

    E.   Locking System: None

    F.   System of Operation: Recoil Operated, Lock Breach

    G.   Maximum Effective Range: 50 meters

    H.   Overall length: 7.7 inches/19.6cm

    I.   Weight unloaded: 1.8 pounds/854g

    J.   Barrel length: 4.6 inches/11.6cm

Figure 1-2 Tokarev (TT) Model 1933 - Tula 1941

Background

Figure 1-3 Fedor Tokarev, TT-33 Designer

Fedor Tokarev (1871-1968)

Fedor Tokarev was the famous Russian weapon engineer who developed a series of pistols called TT (*Tula-Tokarev*, or *Tulskiy-Tokarev*, i.e., Tokarev from Tula, a Russian town which is famous for its weapon-manufacturing plants, known in the US as "Soviet Tula.

The Soviet engineers also added several other features, such as locking lugs all around the barrel (not just on top), and made several alterations to make the mechanism easier to produce and maintain. Production even machined the magazine feed lips into the receiver to prevent damage and misfeeds when a distorted magazine was loaded into the magazine well.

The German army captured TT-33s and issued them to units under the Pistole 615(r) designation. This was made possible by the fact that Soviet 7.62mm Model 1930 Type P cartridges were practically identical to the German 7.63 Mauser cartridges, and thus German ammunition could be used in the captured Soviet pistols.

Production of the TT-33 in the USSR ended in 1954, but copies (licensed or otherwise) were also made by China (as the *Type 51*, *Type 54*, *M20*, and *TU-90*) and Poland. Hungary rebarreled the pistol to fire 9x19mm Parabellum (as the *M48*), as well as an export version for Egypt (the *Tokagypt 58*) which was widely used by police forces. Yugoslavia produced the TT-33 (as the *M57*, *M65,* and *M70A*), as well as North Korea (as the *Type 68* or *M68*). At one time or another most communist or Soviet bloc countries made a variation of the TT-33 pistol, until it was eventually replaced for use by first-line troops by the 8-round, 9x18mm Makarov PM in 1952.

Norinco, the People's Liberation Army's state weapons manufacturer in China, still manufactures a commercial variant of the Tokarev pistol chambered in the more common 9x19mm Parabellum round, known as the Tokarev Model 213, as well as in the original 7.62x25. It features a safety catch, which was absent on Soviet-produced TT-33 handguns. Furthermore, the Model 213 features the thin slide-grip grooves, as opposed to the original Russian wide types. The 9 mm model is featured with a magazine well block mounted in the rear of the magazine well to accept 9mm-type magazines without frame modification. The Norinco model in current production is not available for sale in the United States due to import prohibitions on Chinese firearms, although older handguns of the Model 213 type imported in the 1960s and 1970s are common.

Many Romanian copies of the TT-33 are available in the United States as they have been recently imported.

However, TT served with the Soviet Army well until 1960s, and with the Soviet Militia (Police)- until the 1970s. During the late 1940s and 1950s, USSR also supplied some of its new allies from the Warsaw pact with licenses to manufacture TT, and it was produced in China, Hungary, North Korea, Poland, Romania, and Yugoslavia, in more or less original forms. Most military TT pistols of non-Soviet manufacture were also in 7.62mm, with some commercial export versions available in 9x19mm Luger and fitted with some sort of manual safety.

Variants

http://imageevent.com/willyp/russiansovietcomblocsection/comparisonalbumsofcomblocweapons/tt30tt33tokarevvariants is a great website that catalogs many of the variants.

Type 51/54 (China)

Figure 1-4 Chinese Type 51/54 pistol

Caliber: 7.62x25mm Tokarev and 9x19mm

The Type 54 (Traditional Chinese:54式手槍, Simplified Chinese: 54式手枪), Type 51, M20, TU-90, and Model 213 pistols are Chinese copies of the Soviet-type Tokarev T-33. This type of pistol is commonly available in 7.62x25 mm caliber, although some variants have been made in 9mm Luger. The Model 213 features a safety catch, which was absent on Soviet-produced TT-33 handguns. Furthermore, the Model 213 features the thin slide-grip grooves, as opposed to the original Russian wide types.

M57 (Yugoslavia)

Figure 1-5 Zastava M57 pistol

Caliber: 7.62x25mm Tokarev

The M57 pistol, manufactured by the Yugoslavian Crvena Zastava CZ (Red Banner) factory of former Yugoslavia (now Zastava Arms factory in Serbia), was a standard sidearm of Yugoslavian army. Adopted in 1957, it was a copy of the Soviet Tokarev TT pistol, although the M57 had a longer grip that hosted bigger magazines (9 rounds versus 8 rounds in TT). Around 1970, CZ began production of a similar pistol, chambered for 9x19 Luger ammunition, is known as the M70(d).

The M57 pistol is a short recoil operated, locked breech pistol that uses Browning type action with swinging link. Trigger is of single action type, most pistols have no manual safeties except for a half-cock notch on the hammer but later they put a manual safety on the pistol.

Type 68 (Democratic People's Republic of Korea/North Korea)

Figure 1-6 North Korean Type 68

Caliber: 7.62x25mm Tokarev

This pistol had been developed at state arms factories of DPRK since the late 1960s, and is now in use by the the North Korean army. It is based on the Soviet Tokarev TT, but with certain modifications. This pistol is rarely seen outside of the DPRK.

The Type 68 pistol is a short recoil-operated, locked-breech pistol. It uses a modified Browning-type locking, with the barrel engaging the notches inside the slide with two lugs, machined on the top of the barrel. To lock and unlock upon the recoil cycle, the breech end of the barrel is controlled by the cam-shaped cut in the underbarrel lug (instead of the swinging link found in the original TT pistols). The trigger is of single-action type, with an exposed hammer. There is no manual safety, except for a half-cock notch on the hammer. Single-stack magazines hold 8 rounds and are slightly different from TT magazines by not having the notch on the left side for a TT-type magazine catch. The magazine catch is located at the bottom of the grip. Standard TT magazines can still be used in Type 68 pistols, but not vice versa.

Tokagypt 58 (Manufactured in Hungary for Egypt)

Figure 1-7a FEG Tokagypt 58 pistol, right side

Figure 1-7b FEG Tokagypt 58 pistol, left side

Caliber:	9x19mm
Type:	Single Action
Weight unloaded:	2 pounds/910g
Overall length:	7.6 inches/19.2cm
Barrel length:	4.5 inches/11.5cm
Capacity:	7 rounds

Original Factory Code: TT-9P

Magazine: 7-round detachable box

In 1957 *Femaru Fegyver es Gepgyar* (FEG) received the Egyptian Army contract for a Tokarev TT-33 type pistol in 9x19mm Parabellum. This pistol was developed by Ambrus Balogh, a weapons engineer at Femaru, and was originally referred to as TT-9P, but eventually it was called and marked Tokagypt 58.

It was a significant modification of the Soviet Tokarev TT33 and the Hungarian 48.M for the 9x19mm cartridge. A new safety catch was fitted on the left top side of the receiver, a convenient one-piece wrap-around plastic grip and a finger support on the magazine.

Figure 1-8 Tokagypt 58 proofmarks and the '02' Warsaw Pact country code for Hungary

Figure 1-9 Original contract slide legend with Egyptian crest

Section 2

Maintenance

Figure 2-1 Parts of the TT-33 Pistol

1- Slide Assembly	2- Magazine	3- Barrel Bushing
4- Recoil Spring Guide	5- Recoil Spring	6- Takedown Pin/Slide Stop
7- Barrel	8- Barrel Linkage	9- Frame Assembly
10- Safety (US imports only)	11- Hammer/Sear Assembly	

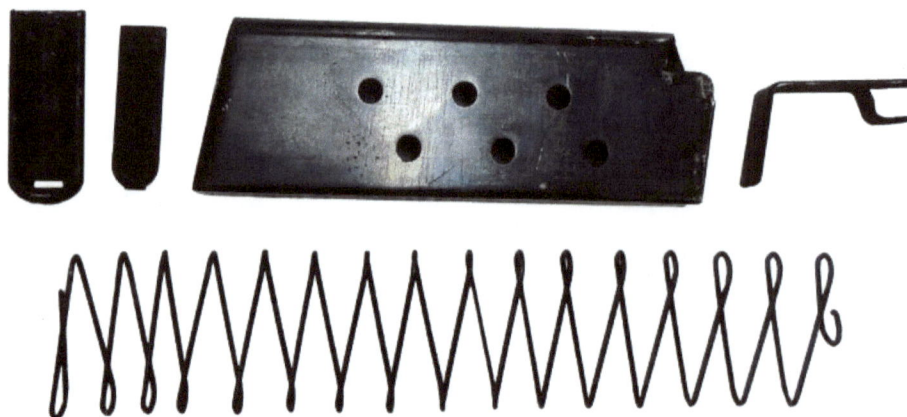

Figure 2-2 Parts of the TT-33 Pistol Magazine

1- Magazine Floor Plate	2- Floor Plate Lock	3- Magazine Body
4- Follower	5- Magazine Spring	

Clearing the TT-33

A. Ensure the pistol is on SAFE (if a US import) and pointed in a safe direction.

Figure 2-3a   **Figure 2-3b**   **Figure 2-3c**

B. Remove the magazine by pressing the magazine catch on the left side of the frame in front of the grip panel and pull the magazine from the magazine well in the grip (Figure 2-3a). You may have to pull on the front lip of the magazine to free it (Figure 2-3b). Place the magazine in a pocket or magazine pouch or set it down (Figure 2-3c).

 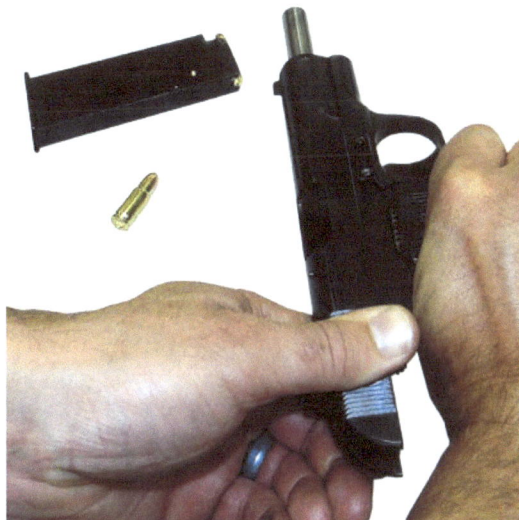

Figure 2-4a   **Figure 2-4b**

C. Grip the serrations on the slide and pull the slide rearward (Figure 2-4a), allowing the round to extract and eject from the pistol, and hold the slide to the rear (Figure 2-4b). Observe the round extracting and ejecting from the ejection port; do not attempt to retain the round.

Figure 2-5

D. Visually check the chamber for rounds (Figure 2-5). Once you have ensured the pistol has no magazine in it and the chamber is free of rounds, you now can close the slide by pulling it to the rear thus releasing the slide stop and riding the slide forward so as not to shut forcefully on an empty chamber.

Disassembling the TT-33 Pistol

NOTE- Place the pistol's parts on a flat, clean surface with the muzzle oriented in a safe direction.

When the operator begins to disassemble the pistol, it should be done in the following order:

A. Clear the pistol and leave the magazine out.

B. To remove the slide,

NOTE: The TT-33's recoil spring is under tension and if not managed correctly, will fly out. Wear eye protection.

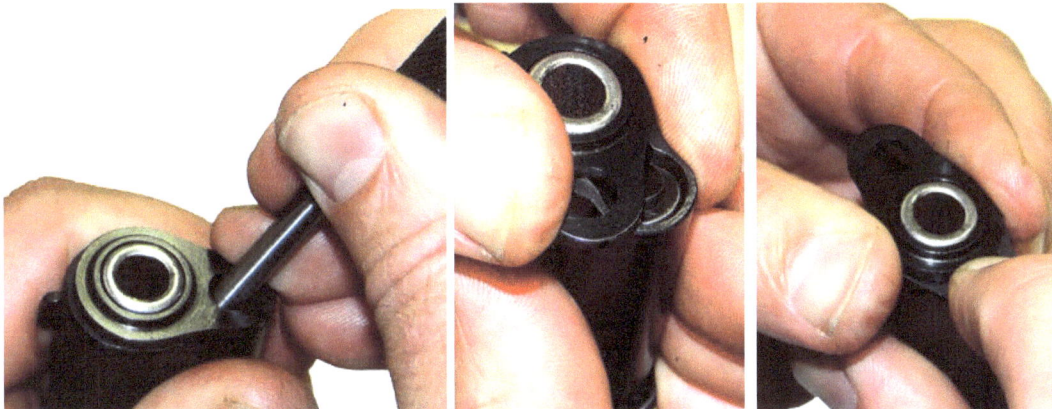

| Figure 2-6a | Figure 2-6b | Figure 2-6c |

1. Using a punch, press down on the recoil spring plug through the bushing (Figure 2-6a). **While continuously pressing down on the recoil spring plug**, turn the barrel bushing clockwise to the 12 o'clock position (Figures 2-6b and 2-6c).

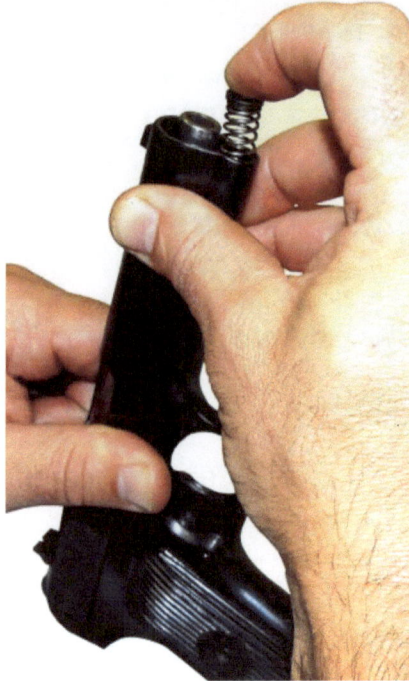

Figure 2-7

2. Remove the barrel bushing. Slowly allow the recoil spring to expand to its fullest extent (Figure 2-7).

Figure 2-8

3. Figure 2-8 shows the direction the flat spring needs to be pushed to remove the slide stop, but do not remove fully if you have the US-import safety installed. With a punch, push the lip of the flat slide stop pin lock so it disengages from the slide top pin.

Figure 2-9

4. Pull the slide stop pin on the left side of the frame towards you, removing it from the slide (Figure 2-9).

Figure 2-10a   **Figure 2-10b**

5. Slide the slide forward and off of the receiver frame (Figures 2-10a and 2-10b).

Figure 2-11

6. Remove the recoil spring assembly and set it aside (Figure 2-11).

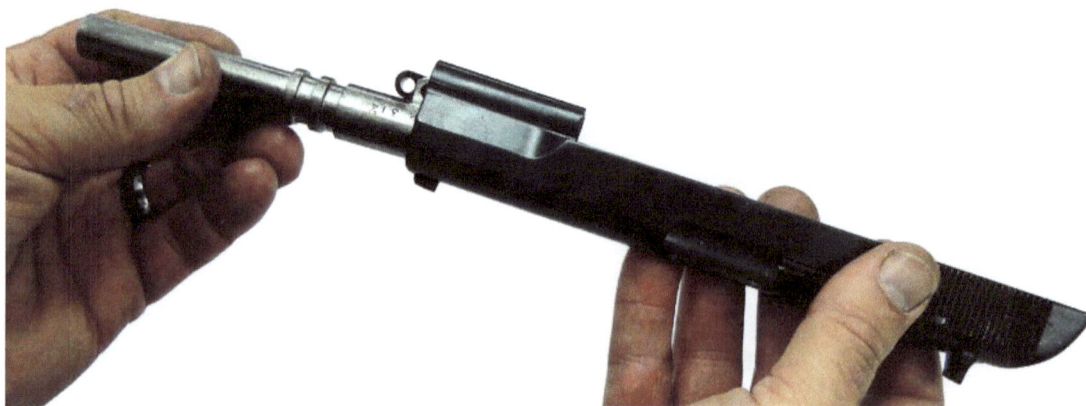

Figure 2-12

7. Push the barrel linkage forward and down as shown (Figure 2-12). Pull the barrel assembly out of the front of the slide. Set the barrel aside.

C. Remove the hammer/sear assembly.

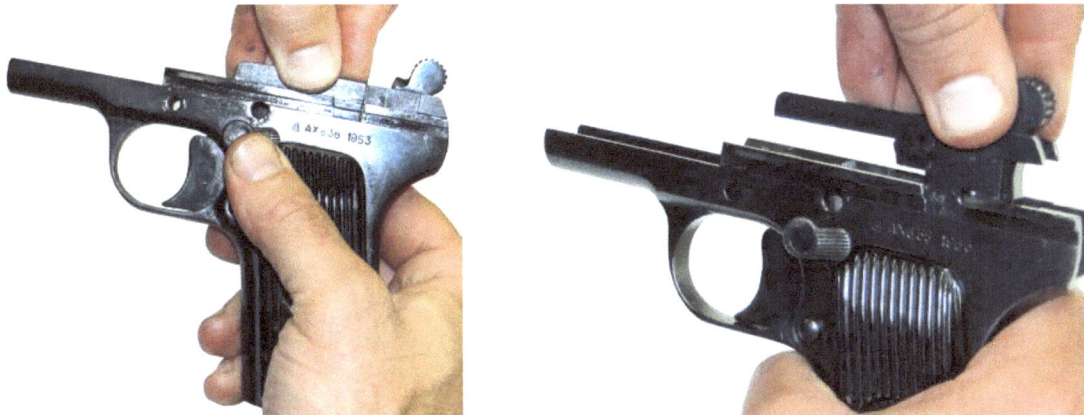

Figure 2-13

8. Grip the hammer/sear assembly. Lift out the hammer/sear assembly and set aside (Figure 2-13).

Figure 2-14 The field disassembled TT-33 pistol

Reassembling the TT-33 Pistol

Figure 2-15a   **Figure 2-15b**

1. Insert the hammer/sear assembly into the frame and set the assembled frame aside (Figure 2-15a). The fully seated hammer/sear assembly (Figure 2-15b).

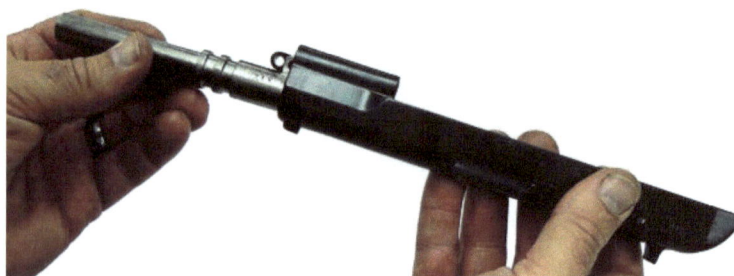

Figure 2-16

2. Slide the barrel assembly into the slide with the linkage down (Figure 2-16).

Figure 2-17

3. Slide the barrel assembly all the way to the rear (Figure 2-17).

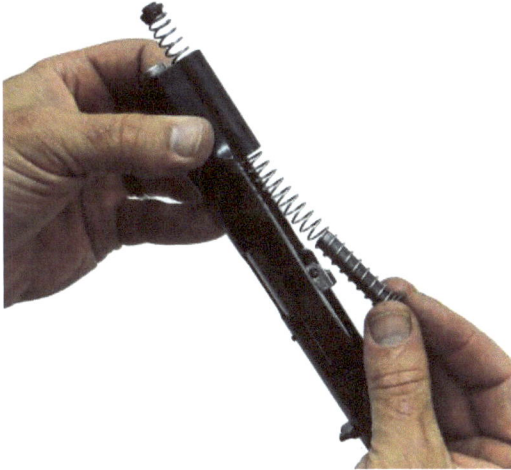

Figure 2-18a   **Figure 2-18b**

4. Insert the bushing pin on the end of the recoil spring/guide assembly through the end of the slide (Figure 2-18a). Lay the recoil spring/guide assembly with the inward curved bottom against the barrel after lifting up the linkage (Figure 2-18b). Figure 2-18b shows how the recoil guide rests upon the barrel.

Figure 2-19a   **Figure 2-19b**

5. While holding the recoil spring guide assembly in place, place the slide onto the frame's rails, Figure 2-19a. Figure 2-19b shows the slide positioned to put in the slide stop pin.

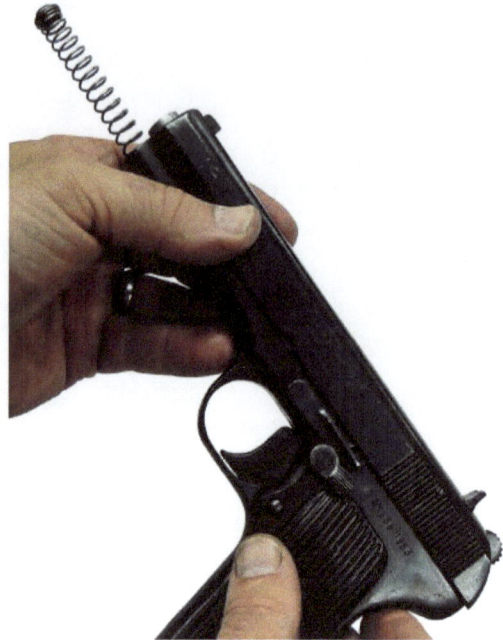

Figure 2-20a   **Figure 2-20b**

6. Align the slide stop pin hole and the barrel linkage hole (Figure 2-20a).
   Insert the pin of the slide stop into the slide stop hole (Figure 2-20b).

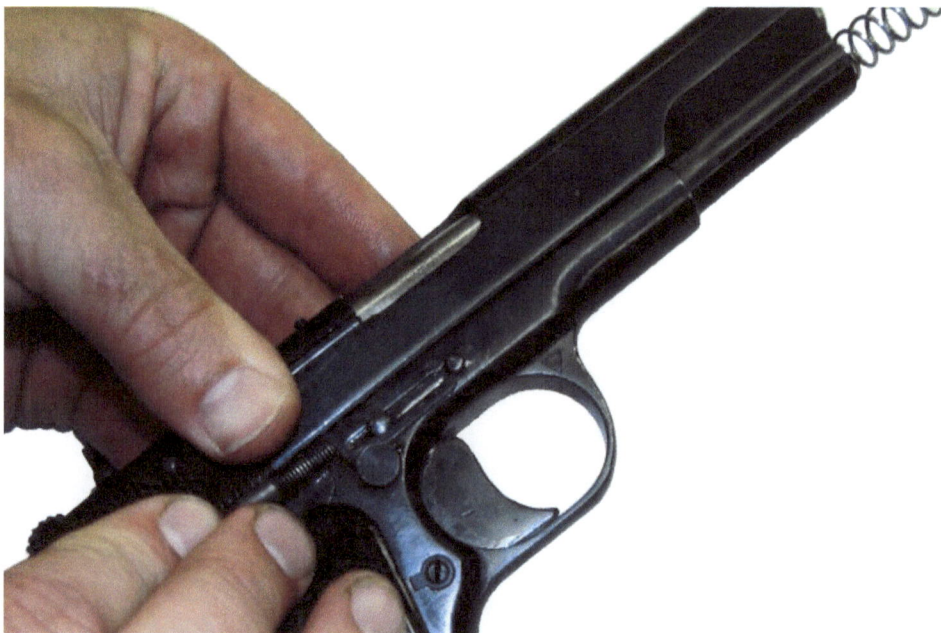

Figure 2-21

7. Slide the flat spring forward so it engages the slide stop pin (Figure 2-
   21).

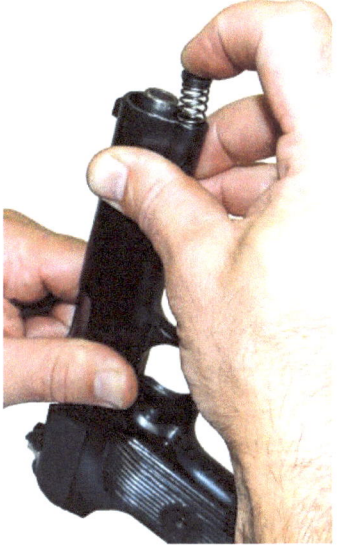 

Figure 2-22a   **Figure 2-22b**

8. Compress the recoil spring and recoil spring plug (Figure 2-22a). While holding the recoil spring plug down, insert the barrel bushing so it is at the 12 o'clock position (Figure 2-22b).

Figure 2-23a   **Figure 2-23b**

9. While continuing to hold the recoil spring plug down, rotate the barrel bushing counter-clockwise (Figure 2-23a) until the barrel bushing locks the recoil spring plug into place (Figure 2-23b).

Figure 2-24 Assembled TT-33 pistol

Performing a Function Check on the TT-33 Pistol

A. Ensure the pistol is clear of ammunition.

B. Pull the slide fully to the rear and allow it to spring forward, the hammer will be cocked.

B. Press the trigger (the hammer will fall).

C. Pull the hammer back to the half-cock notch and press it forward; to ensure it stays engaged.

D. Press the trigger (the hammer should not fall).

Section 3

Operation and Function

Loading the TT-33 Magazine

A. Ensure you have 7.62x25 ammunition. Inspect it for uniformity, cleanliness, and serviceability. Check all cartridges for undented primers and only use issued ammunition.

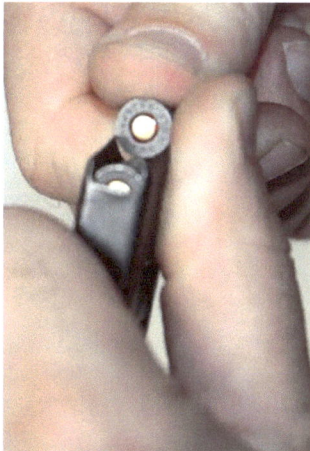 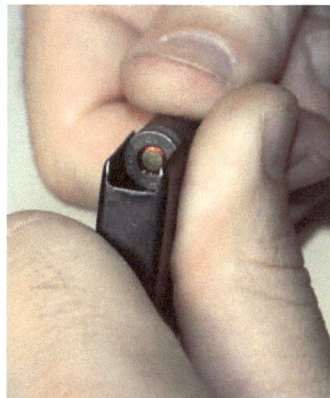 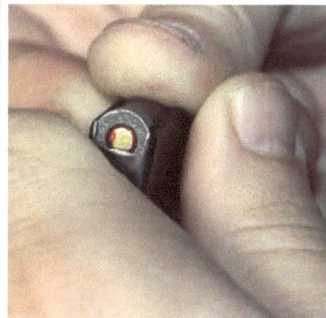

| **Figure 3-1b** | **Figure 3-1b** | **Figure 3-1c** |

B. Use your non-dominant hand to hold the magazine with the rounded front of the magazine towards your fingertips. Your non-dominant thumb is used as a guide so as not to let the cartridge roll off the follower or other cartridges (Figure 3-1a). With your dominant hand, one at a time, begin with the base of the cartridge at the front of the magazine follower and press the cartridge down and back to insert (Figures 3-1b and 3-1c).

C. The magazine can hold seven cartridges, to prevent overloading of the spring, load seven cartridges and then load the chamber so you have six in the magazine and one in the chamber. Placing a cartridge in the chamber and releasing the slide stop can cause damage to the extractor, so load the chamber from the magazine only.

Loading the TT-33 Pistol

A. With the pistol pointed in a safe direction,

B. Insert the loaded magazine into the magazine well. Fully seat the magazine with the heel of the hand to ensure it is locked in by the magazine catch.

C. Pull the slide to the rear by gripping the serrations on the rear of the slide (not over the ejection port) and release, allowing it to slam shut by its own spring tension. To ensure that a round has been chambered either remove the magazine to observe that only six rounds remain or perform a press check to observe the chambered casing through the ejection port. Ensure the slide is in battery (fully forward).

Firing the TT-33 Pistol

A. Orient downrange or towards the threat with your trigger finger off the trigger.

B. Cock the hammer with a thumb.

C. As you orient your sights onto the target, press the trigger straight back so as not to interrupt the sight picture. As the TT-33 is single action, you will notice your first shot and subsequent shots are light (hammer already to the rear).

D. When you have completed firing the pistol, you can unload the pistol to clear it or place the hammer on half-cock.

E. To place a loaded TT on the half notch do the following: Ensure that you retain the hammer with a thumb and forefinger pinch over the slide (Figure 3-2a), press and release the trigger (Figure 3-2b) and ride the hammer forward until the half-cock notch engages (Figure 3-2c). It is not safe to carry the US models with the external safety on and the hammer cocked to the rear.

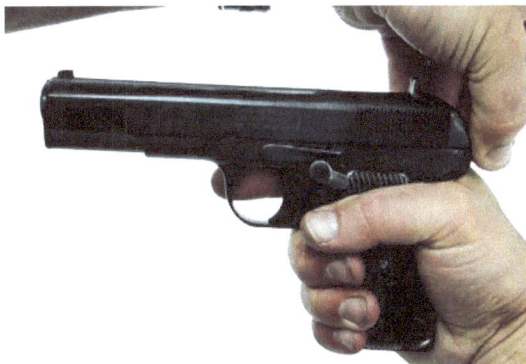

Figure 3-2a

Figure 3-2b

Figure 3-2c

Appendix A - Holsters

Figure A-1a Military-issue holster for TT-33

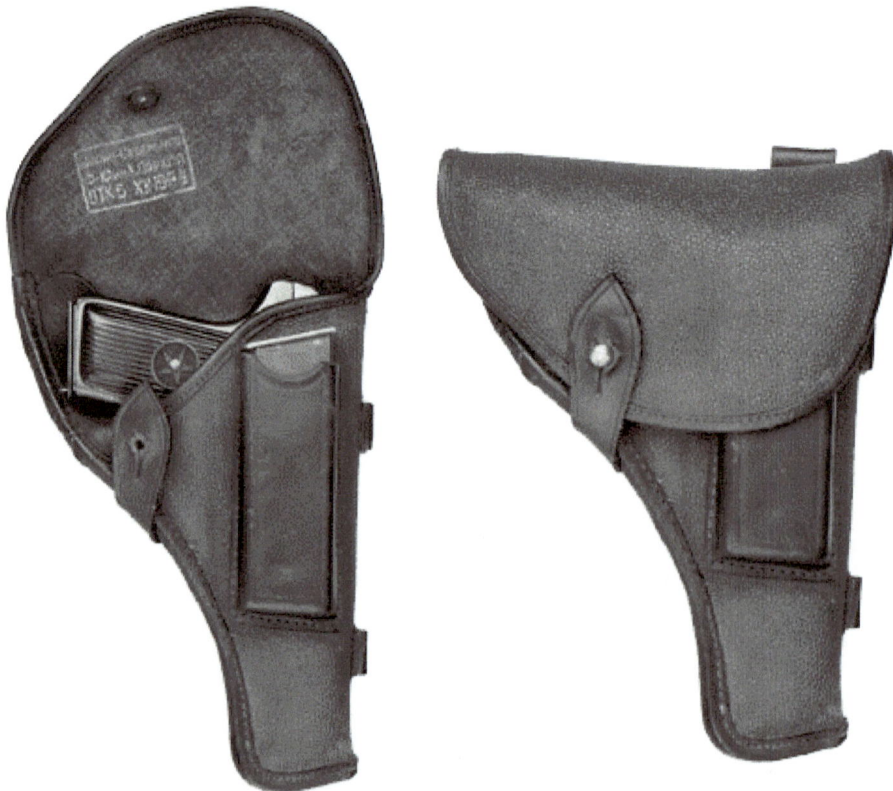

Figure A-1b Military-issue holster for TT-33

Appendix B - Ammunition

7.62x25mm Tokarev

Figure B-1 Side-by-side comparison to other cartridges
From left: .45 ACP, 7.62x25mm Tokarev, 9mm Luger, and 9x18mm Makarov

Figure B-2 7.62x25 mm Tokarev rounds
Left: Standard FMJ Right: Military armor-piercing round

Figure B-3 7.63x25mm Mauser round and 7.62x25mm Tokarev round

The **7.62x25 Tokarev** cartridge is a bottle-necked pistol cartridge widely used in former Soviet and Soviet satellite states. Actual caliber of the bullet is 7.85mm (.309 inches).

Design

The cartridge is basically a Soviet version of the 7.63mm Mauser. They are very similar; in fact, some weapons can use both cartridges interchangeably, though this is not recommended. 7.62 Tokarev is usually much more powerful than its Mauser counterpart and can damage any firearms chambered for 7.63mm Mauser. The Czech version of this cartridge has a 25% higher pressure loading, meaning that it produces significantly more velocity and energy than other common loads and may present a danger to the user when fired from weapons not specifically designed to use it.

The Soviets produced a wide array of loadings for this cartridge for use in submachine guns. These include armor-piercing, tracer, and incendiary rounds. This cartridge has excellent penetration and can defeat lighter ballistic vests (class I and II). Although most firearms chambered in this caliber were declared obsolete and removed from military inventories, some Russian police and Special Forces units still use it for its superior penetration rather than the more popular 9mm Makarov ammunition in current use.

Some firearms that use this round are pistols Tokarev TT-33 and Vz 52 and submachine guns PPD-40, PPSh-41, PPS-43, and K-50 m.

Reloaders have been known to custom load 7.62 x 25mm with .30 caliber sabot rounds with .22 caliber 55 grain (3.6 g) bullets. Muzzle velocities in excess of 2200 ft/s (670 m/s) have been obtained with this method. These speeds are seldom obtained with a handgun; usually, the longer barrel of a rifle is required.

Synonyms

- 7.62mm Type P
- 7.62mm Tokarev
- 7.62x25mm Tokarev
- 7.62x25mm TT
- .30 Tokarev

7.62mm cartridges, type 1930, with a regular bullets

- 7.63mm, Mauser, made in a cartridge factory in the city of Podolsk at the end of the 1920s. The prototype of the cartridge, type 1930.

- 7.62mm, type 1930, lead core and bimetallic-jacketed bullet. Cartridge case - brass.
- 7.62mm, type 1930, lead core and steel-jacketed bullet. Cartridge case - brass. WWII production.
- 7.62mm, type 1930, lead core and steel-jacketed bullet. Cartridge case - steel. WWII production.
- 7.62mm, type 1930, lead core and bimetallic-jacketed bullet. Cartridge case - bimetallic. WWII production.
- 7.62mm, type 1930, with lead core and steel jacketed bullet. Cartridge case steel, brass.
- 7.62mm, type 1930, with lead core and bimetallic jacketed bullet. Cartridge case - bimetallic. Production in the 1950s.

7.62mm cartridges, type 1930, with special bullets

- 7.62mm, type 1930, with armor-piercing + incendiary by bullet P-41. Cartridge case - brass.
- 7.62mm, type 1930, with a tracer bullet. Cartridge case - brass. Production period of WWII.
- 7.62mm, type 1930, with a tracer bullet. Cartridge case - brass. Production-end of the 1940s.
- 7.62mm, type 1930, with a tracer bullet. Cartridge case - bimetallic. Produced up to the 50s.

Auxiliary cartridges

- 7.62mm, type 1930. Dummy cartridge. Made up to the end of the 1940s.
- 7.62mm, type 1930. Dummy cartridge case - brass. Production in the 1950s.
- 7.62mm, type 1930. Dummy cartridge case - bimetallic. Production in the 1950s.
- 7.62mm, type 1930. Technological.
- 7.62mm, type 1930. Blank cartridge case - brass.
- 7.62mm, type 1930. Blank cartridge case - bimetallic.

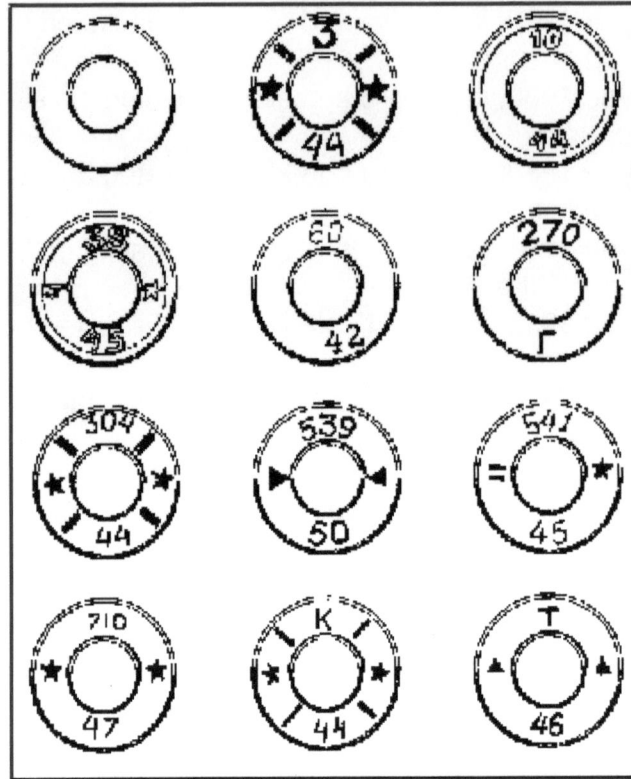

Figure B-4 Factory Head Stamps

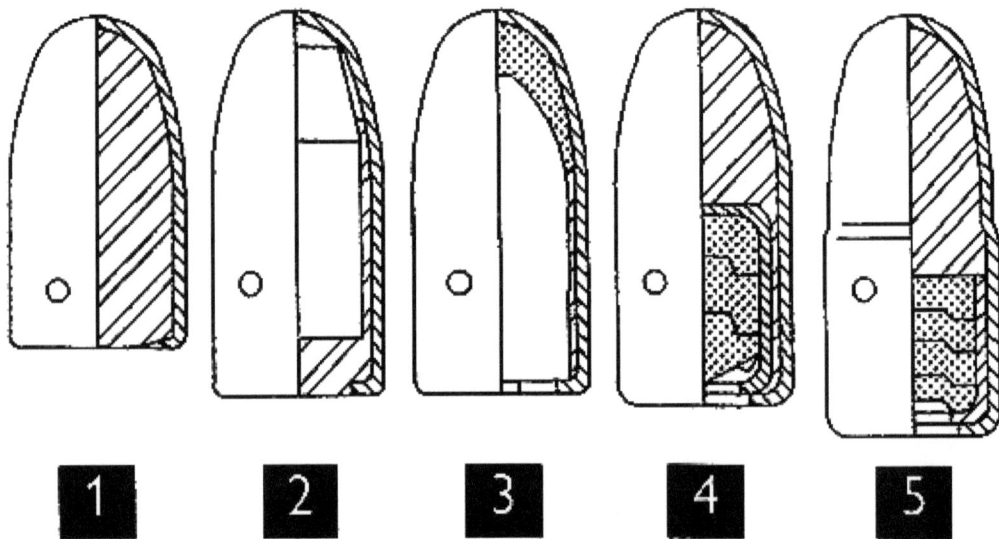

Figure B-5 Sectional View of Bullets

1. Regular bullet with the lead core, "P"
2. Regular bullet with the steel core, "Pst"
3. Armor-piercing + incendiary bullet, "P-41"
4. Tracer bullet, "PT" (production in the 1940s)
5. Tracer bullet, "PT" (production in the 1950s)

At the end of the 1920s, there was a need by the Red Army for a new type of pistol. The alternative between pistols and revolvers was already settled in favor of the pistol. Together with weapon types of diverse design (starting from original models of the designers Korovin, Prilutsky, and Tokarev and foreign pistols Mauser, Walther, and Steyr) domestic versions of ammunition were tested. The cartridge plant in Podolsk at this time made a small amount of cartridges for the pistols Browning, Mauser, Steyr, and some other models. After testing for a standard round, the Mauser cartridge, caliber 7.63mm, was selected for use in a new pistol. Most likely, the purchase had important value for the weapons of the NKVD (People's Commissariat of Internal Affairs), who had plenty of 7.63mm Mauser pistols. For standardization with the existing ammunition caliber, the cartridge was changed to 7.62mm, though the tolerances of the cartridge case and bullet practically had not changed. As for the first cartridges being a copy of the 7.63mm Mauser cartridge, the new 7.62mm ammunition received a bullet of greater diameter than the cartridge of the Nagant revolver, and more ductility of the case, thus permitting the increase of the force of ejection with automatic weapons. The bullet exterior-increase of radius/ogive had also changed, making its nose cone longer, as contrasted to the prototype. With these changes, this ammo was adopted by the Red Army under the title "7.62mm, cartridge for pistols, type 1930."

The difficulties which arose with the development of the pistol "TT" were mirrored in the quantity of ammunition issued for it. Prior to the beginning of the Great Patriotic War, the production of cartridges for TT was limited to a rather small amount. On the cartridge cases made in this period, head stamps are absent. The cartridges were produced only with a regular lead core bullet. The bullet jacket was usually steel, with a tombac plating (an alloy of copper and zinc). A powder charge weight was selected using a calculation for obtaining, at 10 meters, a muzzle velocity of 420-450 mps. It gave a bullet energy of 2070 kg/sm2, at the same distance, equal to 60 kg/m, at a mean maximum pressure, which was not superior. The mean charge weight of P-45/1 smokeless powder (porous), depending on a consignment, lags within the limits of 0.48-0.52 grams. This was applied to equipment and the "VP" powder (Viscose, for Pistols), whose weight oscillated from 0.48 up to 0.6 grams. The grain of the powder P-45/1 was a dark-green color in the form of a short, rather thick cylinder, whereas the grain "VP" represents a thin, long cylinder of greenish color. This powder was used in cartridges made until 1946. The production of this ammunition was sharply increased in the '40s with the beginning of the mass issuing of SMGs.

In 1941, for SMG, the cartridge with the "P-41" bullet was introduced into the inventory. The cartridge came with an armor-piercing + incendiary bullet and well-tried steel core-for defeating enemy personnel and for firing at petrol tanks, motorcycles, automobiles, and airplanes.

The "P-41" bullet, with a weight 4.3-5.1 grams, had a black tip with a red band.

In 1943, a cartridge with tracer bullet "PT," with a weight of 5.2-5.5 grams, was also produced. It gave a bright red line at distances up to 400 meters and was used for indicating targets in combat. The cupola of a the bullet was green in color. The new plants, in addition, were attracted to production of cartridges with a regular bullet and since 1942, placed a head stamp of the manufacturer and year of issue on the cartridge case. And, since 1944, when the productivity of plants reached maximum, large plants, in addition to using steel, put the month of manufacturing on the cartridge. Smaller plants put the quarter date of manufacture on the cartridge case. The increase in the issue of ammunition demanded plenty of scarce materials: brass for cartridge case and bimetal for manufacturing of shell cases. On the other hand, observance of specifications was not required of rigid long-term ammunition storage - they immediately went to the regular army. Such a situation allowed materials to be substituted partially. Four plants out of eight releasing this category of ammunition had run in production cartridges with cheaper bimetallic cartridge cases, and occasionally also steel cartridge cases without a coating. There were bullets with a steel jacket without a coating or plated by brass instead of tombac. Engaging new plants in the manufacturing of cartridges lowered the quality of production. Later, after the ending of the Great Patriotic War (WWII), the remaining ammunition issued up to 1946 was practically completely given away to troops for practice firing or was destroyed. In the post-war time, the production quotas of ammunition were sharply reduced, with many plants starting peace production. Because of a reduction in deliveries of bimetal until 1949, the cartridge was produced only with a brass cartridge case. As of 1949, there was a steel brass cartridge case, the production of which was finished by 1952 with the restoration of the issue of bimetallic cartridge cases soon completely superseding brass. At the same time, modifications were made in the design of a tracer bullet.

The last modernization of the cartridge was in 1955, when instead of the old lead-core bullet, a new one was adopted with the cheaper and solid-steel core. For preservation of the former weight, the length of a bullet was increased up to 16.5 mm. Since 1951, the new bullet, step-by-step, replaced, at miscellaneous plants, production of the old bullet. Except for battle cartridges, cartridges of a secondary role were also produced. During the post-war years, blank cartridges appeared. Instead of a bullet, it had an elongated cartridge case pressed into a "star." Dummy cartridges made prior to the beginning of the 1950s differed from battle ammo by two or three cross-sectional flutes on the cartridge case. Later, cross-sectional flutes were changed to four longitudinal.

Cartridge case with a charge and paper wad instead of a bullet was applied as a burster charge to the flame-thrower ROKS-2. (The wad and bottom of the case for identification were covered with red lacquer.)

The gradual replacement at the end of the 1950s, of the TT pistols with the PM and APS pistols as well as SMGs by AK-47s, at first decreased, and then, in general, eliminated the necessity for production of the 7.62x25mm cartridge.

However, equipment for production was saved at plant 38 until 1989. In the 1970s and in the beginning of the 1980s, special lots of cartridges were produced, on orders of the Army, for export and for certain organizations.

The history of this cartridge is far from completion. Probably, it will become the basis for the creation of modern types of rifles. Confirmation to that is the mention of the 7.62x25mm cartridge in the program for the creation of a prospective pistol for the Russian Army. The interest in the 7.62x25mm cartridge is exhibited by the Ministry of Internal Affairs. Reasons for this are twofold. On the one hand, the widespread occurrence of a means of individual protection has considerably lowered the efficiency 9mm Makarov. On the other hand, in military warehouses, there are huge reserves of 7.62mm cartridges. This fact is especially significant for modern economic considerations.

(From the Russian magazine ***"MasterGun"*** *[МАСТЕР-РУЖЬЕ] #7/8, 1996)*

Appendix C - Ammunition Comparison

9x18mm
Makarov

9x19mm
Luger

7.62x25mm
Tokarev

.45 ACP

PISTOLS AND SUBMACHINE GUNS

Size Comparison of NATO vs. Non-Standard Ammunition

5.56x
45mm

5.45x
39mm

5.56x
45mm

7.62x
39mm

7.62x
51mm

7.62x
54R mm

12.7x
99mm

12.7x
108mm

ASSAULT RIFLES

SNIPER RIFLES & MACHINE GUNS

Appendix D - Non-Standard Ammunition Packaging & Markings

Packaging

Russian small arms cartridges are packed in sealed sheet-metal containers, with two containers per wooden crate. Older Russian production used rectangular containers of heavy gauge galvanized iron with soldered seams. Around 1959, the introduction of painted, rolled edge, rounded corner, tin plate 'sardine can' containers became the standard.

Metal and wooden crates have standardized markings that identify the contents as to caliber, functional type, cartridge case material, quantity and cartridge/powder lot data. Specialized cartridges are further identified by a color code consisting of one or two color stripes which correspond to bullet tip color. AP cartridges with tungsten carbide cores are identified by two concentric circles instead of color stripes. Russian cartridge designation, packaging and marking practices are generally followed by former Soviet-Bloc countries; each, however, has introduced some modifications in designation and marking. Russian ammunition packaging can be distinguished from Bulgarian packaging, which also carries Cyrillic markings, primarily by the different factory codes. The factory code on the container also appears in the headstamp of the cartridges in the container.

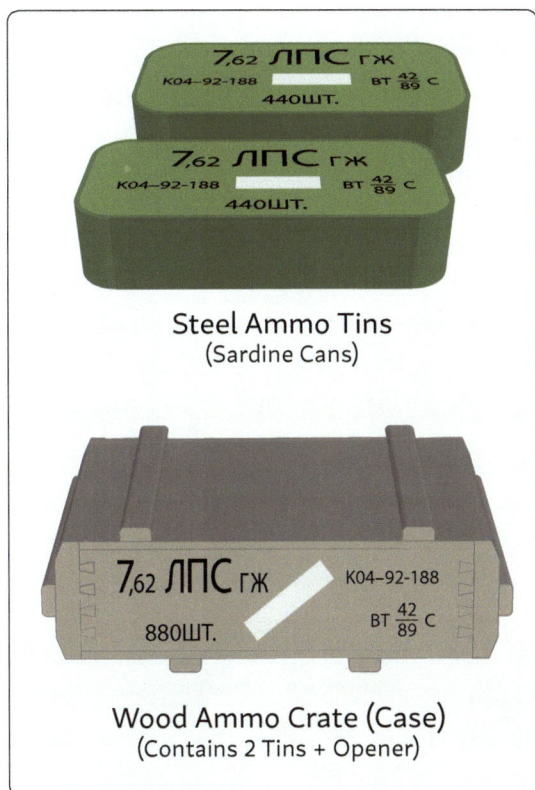

Steel Ammo Tins
(Sardine Cans)

Wood Ammo Crate (Case)
(Contains 2 Tins + Opener)

Cartridge quantities and weights of wooden crates

Country	Manufacturer	Caliber	Rounds /Crate	Crate Weight
Czech Rep.	Sellier and Bellot	14.5 x 114	210	53 kg.
India	OFB	14.5 x 114	60	15.5 kg.
Russia	Unknown	14.5 x 114	80	23 kg.
Bulgaria	Arsenal	12.7 x 108	200	29 kg.
Bulgaria	Arsenal	12.7 x 108	200	32 kg.
Pakistan	POF	12.7 x 108	280	42 kg.
Russia	Unknown	12.7 x 108	190	29 kg.
Russia	Novosibirsk	12.7 x 108	160	25 kg.
Bulgaria	Arsenal	7.62 x 54(R)	880	25 kg.
Czech Rep.	Sellier and Bellot	7.62 x 54(R)	800	24 kg.
Russia	Novosibirsk	7.62 x 54(R)	880	26 kg.
Russia	Novosibirsk	7.62 x 54(R)	600	21 kg.
Russia	Unknown	7.62 x 54(R)	880	26 kg.
Serbia	Prvi Partizan	7.62 x 54(R)	1,200	39 kg.
Czech Rep.	Sellier and Bellot	7.62 x 39	1,200	28 kg.
Pakistan	POF	7.62 x 39	1,750	39 kg.
Russia	Barnaul	7.62 x 39	1,320	30 kg.
Serbia	Prvi Partizan	7.62 x 39	1,260	29 kg.
Sudan	STC	7.62 x 39	1,500	28.1 kg.
Ukraine	Lugansk	7.62 x 39	1,320	30 kg.
Yugoslavia	Igman Zavod	7.62 x 39	1,260	28 kg.
Yugoslavia	Igman Zavod	7.62 x 39	1,120	27.5 kg.
Russia	Unknown	5.45 x 39	2,160	29 kg.
Ukraine	Lugansk	5.45 x 39	2,160	29 kg.

Non-Standard Ammunition tin and crate marking - diagrams

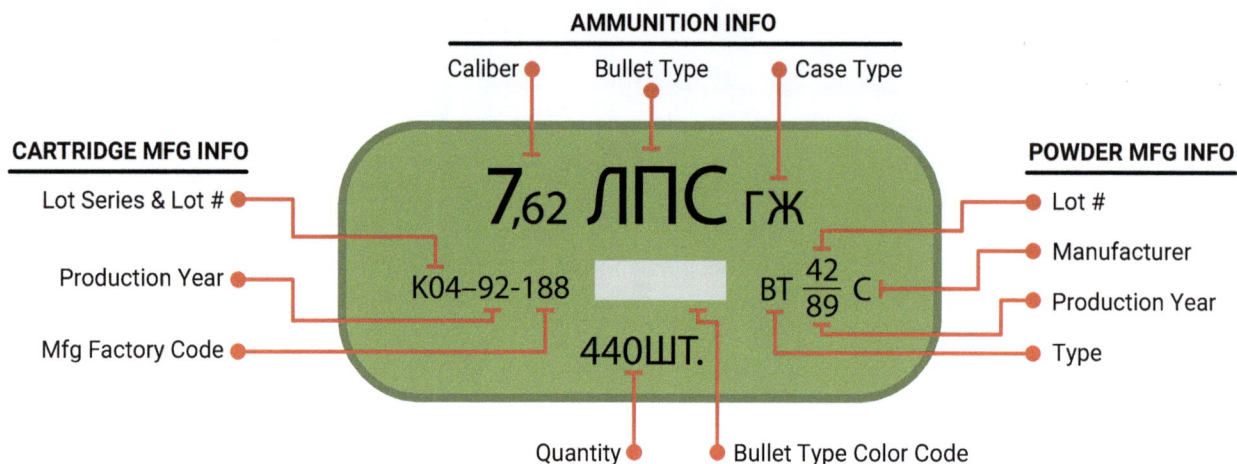

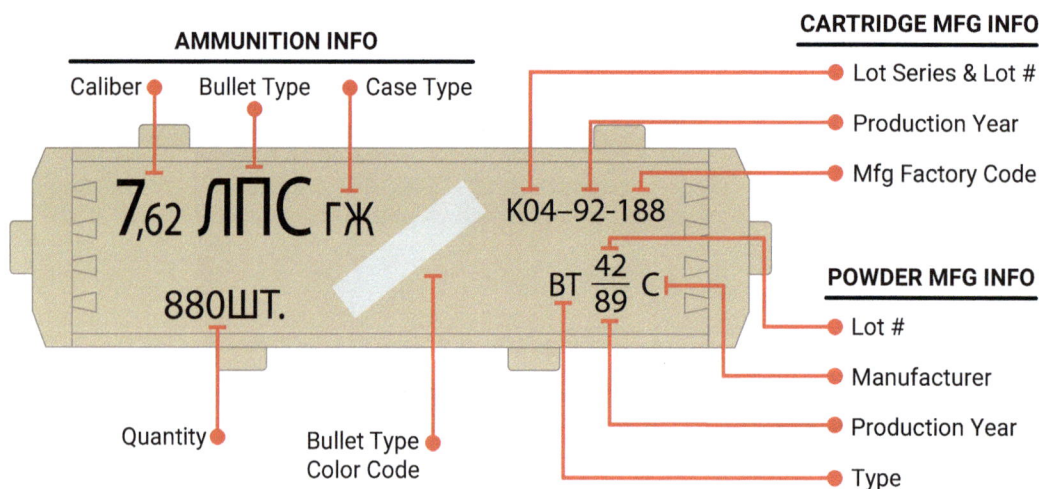

AMMUNITION INFO

Caliber • Bullet Type • Case Type

CARTRIDGE MFG INFO

Lot Series & Lot # •

Production Year •

Mfg Factory Code •

7,62 ЛПС ГЖ

K04–92–188

440ШТ.

BT $\frac{42}{89}$ C

POWDER MFG INFO

• Lot #

• Manufacturer

• Production Year

• Type

Quantity • • Bullet Type Color Code

AMMUNITION INFO

Caliber • Bullet Type • Case Type

7,62 ЛПС ГЖ

880ШТ.

K04–92–188

BT $\frac{42}{89}$ C

CARTRIDGE MFG INFO

• Lot Series & Lot #

• Production Year

• Mfg Factory Code

POWDER MFG INFO

• Lot #

• Manufacturer

• Production Year

• Type

Quantity • • Bullet Type Color Code

Non-Standard Ammunition tin and crate marking - Russian ammunition data

CASE TYPE MARKINGS

Mark	Meaning
ГЖ	Bimetallic case (gilding metal clad steel)
ГЛ	Brass case
ГС	Steel case

CARTRIDGE MFG FACTORY CODES

Code	Location
3	Ulyanovsk
17	Barnaul
38	Yuryuzan
60	Frunze (now Bishkek)
188	Novosibirsk
270	Voroshilovgrad (now Luhansk)
304	Lugansk
539	Tula
711	Klimovsk
T	Tula

Non-Standard Ammunition tin and crate marking - Russian ammunition data

BULLET TYPE MARKINGS

Mark	Meaning
Б Б-30 Б-32 БП	Armor-piercing
БЗ	Armor-piercing incendiary
БЗТ БЗТ-44	Armor-piercing incendiary tracer
БС БС-40 БС-41	Armor-piercing with special core of tungsten carbide instead of carbon steel
БСТ	Armor-piercing with tungsten carbide core with added tracer
БТ	Armor-piercing tracer
Д	Heavy (long-range) with lead core instead of carbon steel
З ЗП	Incendiary
Л	Lightweight bullet
ЛПС	Light ball bullet with mild steel core
МДЗ	High explosive incendiary
П П-41	Spotting / ranging
ПЗ	Incendiary spotting / ranging
ПП	Enhanced penetration
ПС	Spotting / ranging with mild steel core
ПТ	Spotting / ranging tracer
СНБ	Armor-piercing sniper
Т Т-30 Т-45 Т-46	Tracer
57-У-322 57-У-323	Cartridge with higher powder charge
57-У-423	High-pressure cartridge
57-Х-322 57-Х-323 57-Х-340	Blank cartridge
57-НЕ-УЧ	Training cartridge
7Н1	Sniper bullet

BULLET TYPE COLOR CODES (Ammunition up to 14.5mm)

Color	Meaning
No color	Ball
White tip	Reference Ball
Silver tip	Light ball with steel core
Yellow tip	Heavy ball, or ball with torpedo base (on 7.62x54R)
Blue tip + white band	Short range ball 14.5x114 (only Hungarian and Czech)
Green tip + white band	Short range, tracer, (only Czech designation, only found on 7.62x39 with round nose)
Green tip	Tracer
Green tip & head-stamp or entire cartridge green	Subsonic ammunition for silencer-weapons
Red tip	Spotting charge, incendiary
Red tip + white band	Short range tracer ball 14.5x114 (only Hungarian designation)
Entire bullet red	High explosive bullet (7.62x54R after 1945)
Entire bullet red	High explosive bullet (on 12.7 and 14.5mm)
Magenta tip + red band	Armor piercing incendiary tracer
Black tip + red band	Armor piercing incendiary
Black tip + red shell	Armor piercing incendiary with tungsten carbide core
Black tip + yellow band	Armor piercing incendiary Phosphorus 12.7
Black tip	Armor piercing

** The bullet tip color codes in the table above will be the same color codes on the tins or crates, but they will be color stripes on the packaging.

Example:

CARTRIDGE
Black Tip + Red Band

TIN or CRATE
Black Stripe + Red Stripe

Appendix E - Non-Standard Weapon Identification Markings

General Identification Markings

There are various identification markings found on non-standard weapons. Typically the markings will provide some or all of the following information:
- factory name or stamp (proof mark)
- caliber & serial number
- selector lever markings/symbols
- rear sight mark/symbol

NOTE: Data tables are not all inclusive, but they cover the more common weapon manufacturers.

Selector Lever Markings on Kalashnikov Rifles

Upper/ Safe Symbol	Mid/ Full-Auto Symbol	Lower/ Semi-Auto Symbol	Country
	Д	1	Albania
	L	D	Albania
	AB	ЕД	Bulgaria
	L	D	China
	进	单	China
	30	1	Czechoslovakia
	آﻟ	ﺭﺩﻯ	Egypt
	D	E	Egypt
	D	E	East Germany
	∞	1	Hungary
اً	ﺵ	ﻡ	Iraq
	련	단	North Korea
	C	P	Poland
	Z	O	Poland
S	A	R	Romania
S	FA	FF	Romania
	1	3	Romania
	ЛР	ОГОНЬ	Russia
	АВ	ОД	Russia
U	R	ɔ	Yugo/Serbia

Rear Sight Marks on Kalashnikov Rifles

Symbol	Country
D	Albania
П	Bulgaria
D	China
N	East Germany
A	Hungary
卩	North Korea
S	Poland
P	Romania
П	Russia
O	Yugo/Serbia

Non-Standard Weapon Identification Markings

Factory Stamps and Countries of Manufacture

The table of symbols below are factory stamps (proof marks) for non-standard weapons. The symbols will identify the country of manufacture of the weapon. NOTE: *This is not an all inclusive list, but it covers the more common weapon manufacturers.*

⑩ Bulgaria	㉑ Bulgaria	㉕ Bulgaria	China
㊗386 China	△36 China	△66 China	China
Egypt	East Germany	③ East Germany	Ⓚ3 East Germany
East Germany	ⓞ6 East Germany	Iraq	Iraq
☆ North Korea	★ North Korea	⑪ Poland	Romania
Russia	Russia	Russia	Russia
Russia	Russia	Russia	Russia
Yugoslavia/Serbia	M.70.AB2 Yugoslavia/Serbia	ZASTAVA-KRAGUJEVAC Yugoslavia/Serbia	

Appendix F - Non-standard weapons theory overview

There are three key concepts to understand when manipulating non-standard weapons. These simple and logical concepts are:

1. **CYCLE OF OPERATIONS**
2. **OPERATING SYSTEMS**
3. **LOCKING SYSTEMS**

> Firearm design trends are shared across region, manufacturer and class of weapon and are relatively obvious to recognize.
>
> Keep in mind that firearms are essentially simple machines that harness the energy created by the fired cartridge to operate the system.

CYCLE OF OPERATIONS (COO)

The cycle of operations is a crucial basis for understanding how the weapon operates and for function/malfunction diagnosis. Each specific malfunction will correspond to a specific step or sometimes two in the COO. A failure in the system at a certain point, will by default, cause a failure of omission of all subsequent steps. (example – a failure to properly extract will manifest as a failure to eject.)

The COO will vary based on the type of operating and locking systems. Once the operating and locking systems of the weapon are known, the COO is logical.

The examples below all start from a standard reference point: the weapon is loaded, charged, placed on fire and the trigger is pulled.

'Cycle of Operations' Examples:

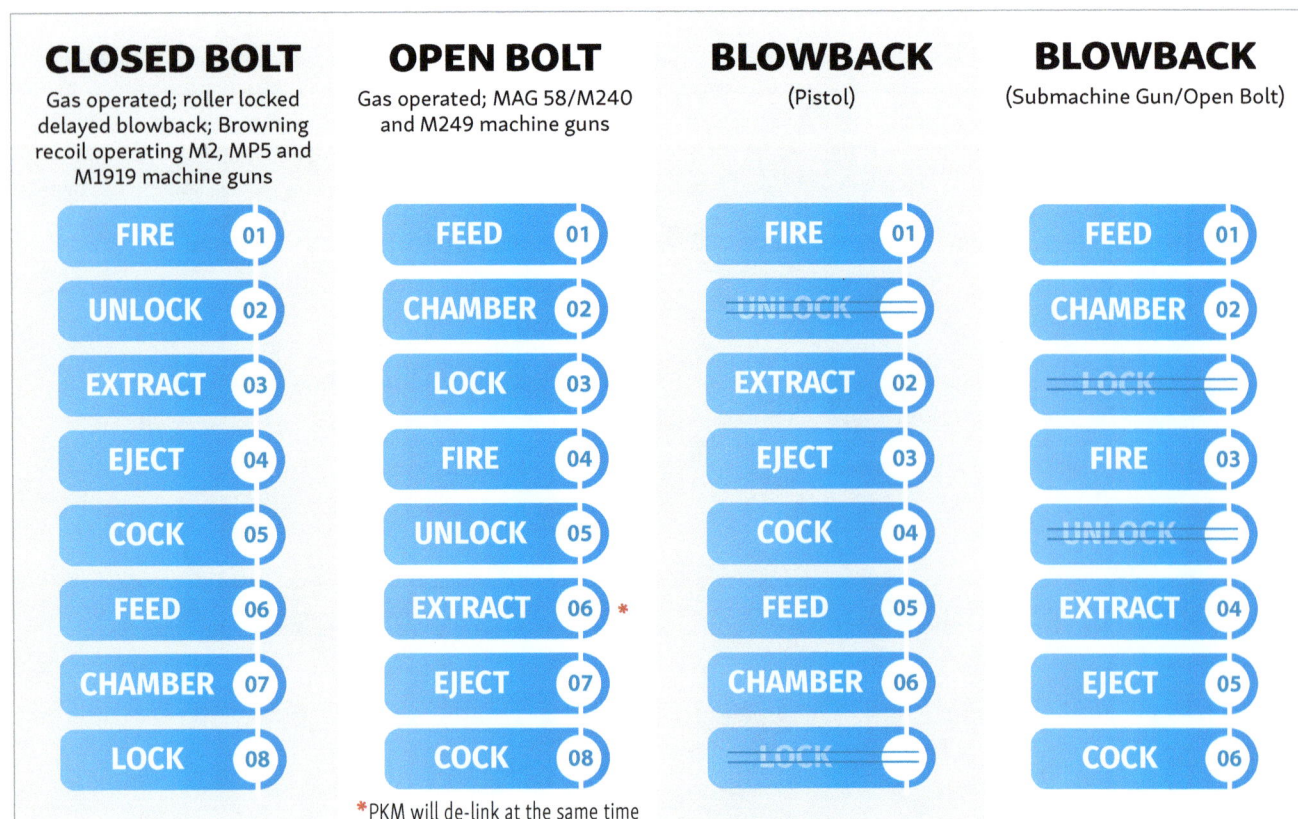

CLOSED BOLT	OPEN BOLT	BLOWBACK	BLOWBACK
Gas operated; roller locked delayed blowback; Browning recoil operating M2, MP5 and M1919 machine guns	Gas operated; MAG 58/M240 and M249 machine guns	(Pistol)	(Submachine Gun/Open Bolt)
FIRE 01	FEED 01	FIRE 01	FEED 01
UNLOCK 02	CHAMBER 02	~~UNLOCK~~	CHAMBER 02
EXTRACT 03	LOCK 03	EXTRACT 02	~~LOCK~~
EJECT 04	FIRE 04	EJECT 03	FIRE 03
COCK 05	UNLOCK 05	COCK 04	~~UNLOCK~~
FEED 06	EXTRACT 06 *	FEED 05	EXTRACT 04
CHAMBER 07	EJECT 07	CHAMBER 06	EJECT 05
LOCK 08	COCK 08	~~LOCK~~	COCK 06

*PKM will de-link at the same time

Non-standard weapons theory overview *(continued ...)*

⚙ OPERATING SYSTEMS

1. **Direct Impingement**- a type of gas operation that directs gas from a fired cartridge directly to the bolt carrier or slide assembly to cycle the action. (AR-15/M4 variants)

2. **Long-stroke piston system**- the piston is mechanically fixed to the bolt group and moves through the entire operating cycle. (AK variants)

3. **Short-stroke piston system (tappet system)**- the piston moves separately from the bolt group. It may directly push the bolt group parts as n the M1 carbine or operate through a connecting rod. (HK 416, AR180, POF, LWRC, FN FAL)

4. **Blowback**- the system of operation for self-loading firearms that obtains energy from the motion of the cartridge case as it is pushed to the rear by expanding gases created by the ignition of the propellant charge. (STEN, Makarov, M3 Grease Gun)

5. **Short recoil action**- the barrel and slide recoil only a short distance before they unlock and separate. The barrel stops quickly, and the slide continues rearward compressing the recoil spring and performing extraction, ejection and finally feeding a fresh round from the magazine in the counter recoil phase. During the last portion of its forward travel, the slide locks into the barrel and pushes the barrel back into battery. *(This is found in most handguns chambered for 9x19mm Parabellum or greater caliber. Smaller calibers, 9x18mm Makarov and below, generally use the blowback method of operation due to lower chamber pressure and associated simplicity of design.)

6. **Roller-locked, delayed-blowback**- when the bolt is closed, the rollers carried in the bolt are wedged into the receiver recesses. On firing, the rollers must be forced out of the recesses at great mechanical disadvantage, delaying the opening of the bolt, even with full power 7.62mm NATO (.308 Winchester) rifle cartridges used in the G3/HK 91 (G3, HK 91, HK 93, HK 53, MP5 variants)

7. **Inertia operated systems**- the bolt body is separated from the locked bolt body to remain stationary while the recoiling gun and locked bolt head moves rearward. This movement compresses the spring between the bolt head and bolt body, storing the energy required to cycle the action. Benelli shotguns.

Non-standard weapons theory overview *(continued ...)*

🔒 LOCKING SYSTEMS

1. **None** - all blowback pistols and some submachine guns – (STEN, UZI, M3 Grease Gun, Makarov, and CZ 82)

2. **Roller** - (HK variants, MG3, MG34, MG 42 and CZ 52)

3. **Rotating bolt** - (AK, Stoner, M60, and M249)

4. **Tilting bolt** - (SKS, FN FAL and MAG 58/M240)

5. **Tilting barrel** - (Tokarev TT33, Sig variants, M1911 variants and Glock variants)

6. **Rotating barrel** - (MAB P15, Colt All American 2000, and Beretta 8000)

7. **Locking flaps** - (RPD, DP/DPM and DShK)

8. **Falling locking block** - (P38, M9, and VZ58)

Function check
Checking the mechanical function of a weapon by replicating, without ammunition, the firing modes from the lowest rate of fire (SAFE if applicable) to the highest in a progressive sequence (not by selector location). The parts checked are the safety/safeties, sear and disconnector.

M4A1
1. Ensure the rifle is clear
2. Charge and place the weapon on SAFE
3. Attempt to fire (weapons should not FIRE, safety is functioning)
4. Place the weapon on SEMI, pull the trigger and hold it to the rear (hammer should fall, trigger/sear functioning)
5. Maintain the trigger to the rear and cycle the bolt
6. Release the trigger and listen for a metallic click (disconnector functioning)
7. Pull the trigger again and the hammer should fall
8. Charge the weapon and place on AUTO
9. Pull the trigger and hold it to the rear then cycle the bolt more than once
10. Release the trigger and pull it again, nothing should happen (auto sear is functioning)
11. Charge the weapon then pull the trigger again and the hammer should fall
12. Function check complete

Significant visual indicators
- Any checked, knurled or serrated surface
- Any movable lever or switch
- Pins with gripping surfaces
- Index marks (two lines that need to be aligned to disassembled (CZ 75)
- Recoil spring with ends of different diameters

www.ingramcontent.com/pod-product-compliance
Lightning Source LLC
Chambersburg PA
CBHW061057090426
42742CB00002B/73